Annie's Message

'Annie's Message' is dedicated to children with
Down's syndrome and their families.

A Word about Down's syndrome

Children with Down's syndrome can do just about anything any other child can do. Though they may have speech delays, take longer to learn new things, they want and need to be part of everyday life. Children with Down's are packed full of personality and often bring out the best in people. They are compassionate, charming and caring with a tendency towards being stubborn and mischievous. There may be times when a sibling is annoyed, bothered, or even embarrassed by their sibling with Down's. Still, with good communication, understanding and a lifetime of shared experiences, deep bonds will form. When given love and encouragement, there's no stopping what any child with any type of disability can do.

Almost every day, Annie tells me I'm her best sister.

"But Annie," I remind her. "I'm your *only* sister."

Annie shakes her head and grins. "No, Emma, you're my *best* sister!"

I smile when she tells me that. I feel the same about her. But it wasn't always that way. I use to get annoyed with Annie, a lot!

But that all changed after the Christmas pageant. Now, if I do badly on a test or miss an easy soccer goal, I'm glad Annie is there to give me a hug.

My sister was born with something called Down's syndrome. "This makes Annie extra special," Mom says.

Down's syndrome gives Annie an upward slant to her eyes, and her face is a little flatter than mine. She learns slowly and needs special education.

Annie learns best by watching me. She follows me everywhere. Even when I am invited to a friend's house!

Though Annie is two years older than I am, she's two grades below me. Sometimes it's kind of tough to be the older sister . . . to my older sister.

Annie's warm smile could melt an iceberg. But when Annie gets an idea in her head, she is strong like an iceberg, too. Nothing can convince her to change her mind then. Some days Mom calls her "strong-willed Annie" a lot.

I try to reason with Annie when she gets a *strong* idea. But it doesn't always help.

Like when Annie insists, orange is prettier than pink. Or, she wants me to agree that dogs are better than cats.

"You're impossible!" I tell her.

I felt that way before the school Christmas pageant.

I was finally old enough to try out for the part of Mary, the mother of Jesus. The most prized role of all!

After tryouts, I ran home, eager to tell Mom and Dad the good news. Of course, they were pleased I got the part. And they were just as pleased that Annie was asked to be one of the angels.

One night I was practicing my serene look when Annie enters my room.

"Please get out," I tell her. "I'm practicing, and I don't want you bothering me."

Annie sits on my bed, *anyway*. She insists on helping.

"You're ruining my concentration," I say. Our eyes meet in the mirror.

Annie pats the doll in my arms. "You're lucky, Emma," she said. "You get to hold the baby. I wish I could hold Baby Jesus, too."

"Annie, it's just a doll in the manger," I tell her. " It's not really Jesus."

"Besides," I manage a smile. "You're going to be an angel this year. That's pretty special too!"

"What do angels do?" Annie wants to know.

"Angels help people," I answer. "You like helping people don't you."

Annie smiles and sings "Away in a Manger," a song she's learning for the play. She has a sweet voice, but I start to worry. I don't want anything to go wrong.

On the night of the play, Annie's golden tinsel halo keeps falling off.

"Annie, please sit still so I can pin the halo back into place," Mom says calmly.

Annie frowns. She does not like having her hair brushed. "You're hurting my hair!" she wails.

I had enough of Annie's nonsense. "It's just hair, Annie. You can't hurt hair!"

Dad comes to the rescue. "Who wants an ice cream sundae after the play?"

Annie *finally* sits still. Ice cream is her favorite treat. Especially strawberry sundaes!

We arrive at the school, and the chairs were starting to fill. The auditorium buzzes like a beehive on a hot summer day.

I felt as though popcorn was popping inside my stomach. My hands feel like ice. Mom looks at me with a worried look.

I begin to wish I hadn't tried out for the play. "What if I can't remember my lines?" I whisper.

Mom puts her arm around me and looks deep into my eyes.

"You'll do fine, Emma. I know you will," Mom says. "Remember the reason for the season."

The orchestra tunes their instruments, and Joseph repeats his lines. Angels scurry about until all find their place.

With the lights dimmed, the director, Mr. Withers, brings a woman onto the stage. In her arms is a sleeping baby.

"This is Mrs. Harris." Mr. Withers tells me. "We thought it would be nice to have a real baby."

Mrs. Harris carefully places the sleeping baby into the manger bed. "I just fed him," she said. "Micah should sleep right through the program."

A real baby! I was feeling kind of grown-up and . . . a little scared, all at once.

Paul, the narrator, begins by telling how the first Christmas night began so long ago.

Yes, everything was going perfectly.

While the angels sing a greeting to the shepherds, I glance over at my sister.

Annie was singing with all her heart. Like air coming out from a balloon, I breathe out a big sigh of relief.

I look at the sleeping child. He was kind of sweet with his eyes closed.

"Bah!" A boy dressed as a sheep makes loud braying noises. Micah stirs and tries to move his arm.

As I loosen the blanket, Micah's eyes open. He looks surprised. Suddenly, he lets out a wail. In an instant, footsteps stomp across the wooden stage.

Annie is marching toward me with a big smile on her face!

I hear giggles rise from the audience—my heart races. My face feels hot. *Why did Annie have to be this way! Why!*

Annie looks at the baby in the manger. "Hey, he's alive!" she calls out. "He's alive."

I try to tell Annie to head back to the choir, but no words come out. I couldn't talk.

Annie sits down . . . right next to me. Seeing the radiant angel smiling down on him, the baby laughs.

Someone in the audience whispers, "What did the angel say?"

Someone answers. "He's alive!"

Then, like ripples in a pond, "He's alive,' echoes throughout the crowd."He's alive . . . He's alive . . . He's alive!"

When the lights come back on, all stand and sing "Joy to the World." It sounded thunderous!

Annie stays next to the baby for the rest of the play. After the play, Mrs. Harris places the baby in Annie's arms.

Annie was thrilled!

Everyone agrees the play was made extra special because of Annie's *message*.

"You were a wonderful angel, Annie," Mrs. Harris said.

"Emma, you were a lovely Mary," I was told again and again.

But I thought about the gift. The gift Annie had given. Just like the angels on the first Christmas, my sister reminded everyone that the best Christmas gift of all was Jesus, God's Son.

Annie pressed her warm, sticky hands into mine. "I love baby Jesus, Emma."

I give Annie a long hug. "You were the best angel in the play," I tell her.

But there was something more I had to say. I look deep into Annie's eyes. "You are my best sister, Annie. And I wouldn't trade you for anything in the whole world."

www.ingramcontent.com/pod-product-compliance
Lightning Source LLC
Chambersburg PA
CBHW060839270326

41933CB00002B/138

* 9 7 8 0 9 8 1 3 4 1 7 4 3 *